Introduction to

A BETTER WAY

TO PRAY

D0710944

Andrew Wommack

Published in partnership between Andrew Wommack Ministries and Harrison House Publishers.

Woodland Park, CO 80863 - Shippensburg, PA 17257

ISBN 13 TP: 978-1-5954-8526-7

For Worldwide Distribution, Printed in the USA

1 / 26 25 24 23

Contents

Introduction

When the disciples asked Jesus how to pray, our Lord confronted the myths and misconceptions concerning prayer in His day. In fact, He spent quite some time countering false ideas and discussing what prayer is not before He told them the proper way to pray. The religious system had become so hypocritical and phony that the Lord had to undo what they commonly thought prayer was before He could effectively teach them what it is.

The title of this book is neither *The Only Way to Pray* nor *You Won't Get Any Results If You Don't Pray This Way*, but rather **A Better Way to Pray**. In this booklet, I share some things that might offend you. But let me ask you this: If the way you are praying isn't getting good results, why would you resist change in this area? Rest assured that if I step on your toes, the Lord will heal them!

Everything I'm teaching against here, I've done. God still loved me, and I loved Him. We had a good relationship despite the fact that I was doing these things. However, I am now much more

1

effective in seeing manifestations of my answered prayers than ever before in my life.

I'm not the perfect example. I haven't arrived—but I've left. I believe what the Lord has revealed to me through His Word will really bless you. Even though it may be different from anything you've ever been taught before, I'm confident you'll find it—*A Better Way to Pray*!

Chapter 1

Hypocrites Love to Pray

Prayer is the most abused part of the Christian life today. Misguided understandings about it have messed more people up spiritually than anything else! This is why I believe Jesus taught what prayer is not before He taught what it is (Matt. 6:5–13). If He hadn't countered the religious concepts concerning prayer, the people would never have been able to grasp what it actually is. First of all, He revealed that hypocrites love to pray:

> *And when thou prayest, thou shalt not be as the hypocrites are: for they love to pray standing in the synagogues and in the corners of the streets, that they may be seen of men. Verily I say unto you, They have their reward.*
>
> Matthew 6:5

Most believers don't associate hypocrites with prayer. They think, *If you're praying, what could be wrong?* Plenty! Just because you start with the words "Our Father" and conclude with "Amen" doesn't mean it's biblically sound prayer.

The Pharisees of Jesus' day had made prayer a religious calisthenic. Today people use it to soothe their consciences, or they do it to manipulate and motivate God to move on their behalf. Wrong, wrong, wrong.

The heart attitude behind your prayer interests God much more than the actual words you say. Just because you spend an hour—or more—in what you call "prayer" doesn't mean you're accomplishing anything. If your attitude is wrong, you're praying wrong!

If you aren't seeing the desired results from your prayer life, check your motives. If you don't have the proper heart attitude, it doesn't matter what you do. Praying in tongues, prophesying, having faith, giving your possessions to the poor, or even laying down your life will all profit you nothing if they're done without God's kind of love (1 Cor. 13:1–3).

> **The heart attitude behind your prayer interests God much more than the actual words you say.**

God Already Moved

Most Christians see prayer as an opportunity to "move God." They believe He can do anything but that He won't do much until they pray. In this mentality, they use prayer like a crowbar to, in a sense, pry the windows of heaven open and make Him do something. If this is what you believe, your prayer life rests on an extremely faulty foundation. Prayer isn't how you twist God's arm to do something; it is receiving by faith what He has already done!

Someone will ask, "What has God done?" Everything He's ever going to do! He moved once and for all in the death, burial, and resurrection of Jesus Christ. Through the atonement, God has already forgiven and healed every person who will ever be forgiven or healed. He no longer has to lift even His little finger to cause a healing or salvation.

> **Prayer isn't how you twist God's arm to do something; it is receiving by faith what He has already done!**

As far as God's concerned, the sins of the entire world have already been forgiven (1 John 2:2). The Lamb's perfect sacrifice dealt decisively with the past, present, and future sins of every believer and nonbeliever alike. This doesn't mean that all are just "automatically" saved (or healed). God's Word clearly proclaims, *"As ye have therefore received Christ Jesus the Lord, so walk ye in him"* (Col. 2:6). Each individual must receive for themselves by faith what Jesus Christ has provided. A gift given isn't enjoyed until it's received.

In the same way that you appropriate and walk in forgiveness of sin, you receive healing, deliverance, prosperity, and everything else! Christ already made full provision for the abundant life through His atonement. It's not up to Him now to do it, but it's up to you to receive it.

It's Jackhammer Time!

The greatest manifestation of God's power came when you were born again. By nature, you were a child of the devil. He had legal rights and claims to you. As a citizen of the kingdom of darkness, the enemy legitimately dominated your life. At the time of your salvation, you hadn't been fasting, praying, studying the Word, attending church, paying tithes, or living a holy life. Yet without any such effort, you received the greatest miracle of all. It happened because you believed it was already done. How could you doubt that God would do what He had already done?

The Gospel is good news (what God's done) not the "good prophecy" (what He's going to do)! "News" in a newspaper has taken place in the past. The question isn't "Will God save you?" but "Will you accept His salvation?" The gift has been given, but will you receive it?

Before Jesus taught what prayer is, He revealed what it is not. Let's take a jackhammer to our faulty foundations and throw them out—they're only hindering us anyway!

Chapter 2

How Long Do You Pray?

Most people basically believe that the longer they pray, the better it is, and the more God will answer. So, they conclude that praying longer is the solution to everything. Friend, there is absolutely no virtue in long prayers.

Prayer becomes religious when you try to use it for something God never intended. You can promise Him, "I'm going to pray an hour a day if it kills me!" and then do it for a week, or a month or two. But it never lasts, because that's not the way He's leading you. Don't fool yourself into thinking you'll be heard by praying long periods of time or using certain words to petition Him again and again and again. The Lord made it very clear that this isn't what prayer is (Matt. 6:7).

Constant Communion

Some people try to make their relationship with God be this constantly spectacular thing. They think they must be screaming at the top of their lungs, kneeling, hands held high, tears rolling down their cheeks, lightning bolts flashing, and thunder crashing all around in order to really be "in communion with God." If that's what you consider "prayer," you're never going to prosper.

Prayer is communion with God! It's fellowship, relationship, and intimacy with Him. It's conversation. Prayer is both talking and listening. Ninety-five percent of the time I spend in prayer, I'm just thanking, loving, praising, appreciating, and hanging out with the Lord—nothing special or dramatic. The vast majority of prayer is simply visiting with God!

The expression of this communion isn't about how loud you are or a particular set of body positions. In the Bible, people knelt, raised their hands, and even looked up into heaven at times, but don't make these things a requirement in order to consider something "prayer." It doesn't have to be that way to please God. You can

> **The vast majority of prayer is simply visiting with God!**

pray with your eyes open or closed, hands raised or down, standing, kneeling, or prostrate. Since meditation is prayer (Ps. 5:1), you don't even have to talk out loud! Your communion with God should be constant. You should be able to pray while you're driving down the street (eyes open, of course!), working, maintaining your house, doing laundry, etc. Be creative and find ways to commune with Him all day long!

Do you know how to appreciate God in the small things? Are you always trying to do something earthshaking or monumental to build your intimacy with Him? You can't sustain your relationship that way! Adam and Eve walked in the cool of the garden with God. I'm sure their conversations consisted of: "Father, I saw a flower today that I've never seen before. You did a great job!" That's prayer. It's communion with God. Don't miss out on who the Lord is by making your relationship with Him too intense!

There have been times when I've stood and taken authority over the devil, done warfare, bound and loosed, and seen miracles happen because of it; but all of this is just a tiny part of my prayer life as a whole. Yet, these things are normally taught as if they are so very important. People hear me minister on prayer as primarily loving God and immediately respond, "Oh, no, that's too simple. We need to be strong in prayer by regularly doing all of these other things!" I totally disagree.

Most teaching on prayer today centers on how to request and receive something from God. It's all about getting your prayers answered and, if you're really spiritual, how to receive answers for other people too (i.e., intercession). Although it's appropriate to ask for your needs to be met (John 16:24), this should only be a very small part of your prayer life.

> **Asking and receiving is *one* purpose of prayer, but it's definitely not *the* purpose of prayer.**

If it's your primary focus, then it's also one of the main reasons why your prayers aren't very effective. Asking and receiving is *one* purpose of prayer, but it's definitely not *the* purpose of prayer. God wants to meet your needs, but seeking to receive something from Him should not dominate your prayer life.

If you made the main thing the main thing in prayer—loving, worshiping, and fellowshipping with God—you would soon discover that you don't have as many needs! When you seek first God's kingdom, things are just supernaturally added to you.

Therefore I say unto you, Take no thought for your life, what ye shall eat, or what ye shall drink; nor yet for your body, what ye shall put on. Is not the life more than meat, and the body than raiment?

Matthew 6:25

Lost people are completely occupied with the pursuit of what to eat, what to wear, where to live, etc., but believers shouldn't be that way. God is fully aware of your need for these physical things, but He's commanded you to *"seek ye first the kingdom of God, and his righteousness."* As you do, *"all these things shall be added unto you"* (Matt. 6:33). When you're passionately in love with God, He takes care of you—supernaturally—better than you could ever take care of yourself!

By literally living to love Him, you release powerful spiritual dynamics that positively affect the flow of provision in your life.

Most people can't wrap their brains around this truth because it's simply too far outside their realm of experience. It just floats right over their heads! I'm not talking about making your family or career the main thing and loving God on the side, or merely having Him add an "extra quality" to your lifestyle. I mean God is your complete focus—the very center of your life.

For an average Christian, the Lord is just another addition to their already busy life. Their focus is on making a living, raising the kids, maintaining their residence, acquiring more creature comforts, and doing many other temporal activities. On the side, they try to add God into the mix, but He's definitely not the center. They work their tails off because the burden of producing wealth remains on their shoulders. Stressed out, they constantly struggle with worry because they're the ones always trying to make ends meet.

However, when God is truly the center of your life, everything else works out. The Lord makes it work—supernaturally. I can't explain how, but it's a kingdom principle. When God prospers you, it's effortless. Yet, I've met very few Christians who are truly in this divine flow. When your whole heart is simply "God, I love You!" you'll find that He has many ways of working things out.

Chapter 3

What Christianity Is All About

Since most believers are ignorant of that divine flow, they aren't enjoying a very intimate relationship with God. The whole Christian life—specifically prayer—has been reduced to "How can I make God do this? How can I receive that from God? How can I make Him do this for someone else?" We aren't using prayer for what it's really for!

Prayer is communion and fellowship with God. It's saying, "Father, I love You!" and hearing Him answer, "I love you too!" It's listening to Him in your heart and feeling His pleasure as you spend time with Him. If you did that, you wouldn't have to spend much time asking for things, because they'd just supernaturally show up.

The Word reveals that all of God's blessings should be coming upon us and overtaking us (Deut. 28:2). I haven't seen very many Christians with blessings chasing them, but there sure are lots of believers out chasing blessings! The Christian life is a painful, difficult struggle when 95 percent of your prayer life is

> **If loving and communing with God isn't our primary purpose in prayer, we're missing out on what Christianity is all about!**

asking for things, repenting, bawling and squalling, griping and complaining, telling God what the doctor said, informing Him of your bills, and such. If loving and communing with God isn't our primary purpose in prayer, we're missing out on what Christianity is all about!

God Wants You!

God isn't as concerned about what you do as He is who you are. He wants your fellowship more than your service, but the church has emphasized, "Do a work for God!" We've equated His love and acceptance of us to be proportional to how well we think we're performing. We've become "human doings" instead of "human beings." We feel obligated and duty bound to "serve Him" because we feel we "owe" God. This debtor mentality is what gives us the concept, "I have to do something for God."

> *Thou art worthy, O Lord, to receive glory and honour and power: for thou hast created all things, and for thy pleasure they are and were created.*
>
> Revelation 4:11

You were created for God's pleasure! He loves you and wants to show you how much He loves you so you could then say, "I love You too!" That's what God created you for, not just to do something. It's true He wants things done, but your service is a byproduct of your intimate relationship with Him.

Praying: Public vs. Private

But thou, when thou prayest, enter into thy closet, and when thou hast shut thy door, pray to thy Father which is in secret; and thy Father which seeth in secret shall reward thee openly.

Matthew 6:6

People have actually challenged me before, contending, "You should never pray in public!" Well, Jesus prayed in public. The parallel of this passage begins in Luke 11:1 when Christ's public praying caused the disciples to say, *"Lord, teach us to pray."* If the Lord literally meant to always pray in secret so that nobody ever heard you, then He didn't follow His own instructions. Remember, in Matthew 6:5, Jesus basically declared, "Don't be like the hypocrites who pray for the attention and recognition of people."

It's appropriate to isolate yourself alone with God for special times of intimacy—but not all of the time! You must learn to pray in the midst of your daily responsibilities and weekly routines because they occupy the majority of your life. Walk and talk with Him all day, every day!

God wants each of us to mature to the point where we can enjoy just hanging out with Him. He desires our fellowship when there's nothing being said and nothing specific happening other than being together and loving each other.

When I pray for longer periods of time, a significant portion is usually spent praying in tongues. I'm not so much petitioning God as I am promoting my own spiritual growth. I'm praying for and receiving wisdom and revelation from the Lord. Self-edification is an important New Testament purpose of prayer (1 Cor. 14:4 and Jude 20–21).

I also like to build my relationship with God through studying Scripture. Reading the Bible is prayer to me because I do it with my heart, not just my head. When I'm fellowshipping with God, one scripture can occupy me for hours! As I meditate, ask questions, and let Him speak, revelation comes. This is prayer!

Don't Beg God—He Already Knows!

But when ye pray, use not vain repetitions, as the heathen do: for they think that they shall be heard for their much speaking. Be not ye therefore like unto them: for your Father knoweth what things ye have need of, before ye ask him.

Matthew 6:7–8

Many Christians picture in their minds a huge desk in heaven piled high with millions of prayers for God to process. They assume

He's swamped, and it might take Him months to get to their request. Therefore, they take it upon themselves to inform Him of their urgency, praying, "You need to get to this one quickly!"

> **Prayer is not to inform "poor misinformed God" about how bad your situation is!**

They hope He'll then move their request up to the top of the pile and stamp "approved" on it. This mental image and its related attitudes are completely wrong. God is not bogged down, months behind, or unaware of your urgency. Prayer is not to inform "poor misinformed God" about how bad your situation is! He already knows what you need—even before you ask!

In Luke 11:5–8, Jesus shared a parable that's commonly used to teach prayer; however, what's most often taught is exactly the opposite of what the Lord meant:

> *And he said unto them, Which of you shall have a friend, and shall go unto him at midnight, and say unto him, Friend, lend me three loaves; For a friend of mine in his journey is come to me, and I have nothing to set before him? And he from within shall answer and say, Trouble me not: the door is now shut, and my children are with me in bed; I cannot rise and give thee. I say unto you, Though he will not rise and give him, because he is his friend, yet because of his importunity he will rise and give him as many as he needeth.*

This passage is commonly taught that God is comparable to this "friend." You must go to Him when you have a need, but when you first ask for it to be met, He may answer "No!" or "I'm not ready." Therefore, you must stay after God, badgering Him and persistently praying your request over and over again until you make Him give you what you need. Sometimes this is called "importunity in prayer." Basically, you must bombard the gates of heaven until they "open."

However, Jesus was making a contrast not a comparison! The Lord used this physical example to show that if a friend would treat you better than this, why would you think God must be badgered, begged, and pled with to meet your need? Why would your heavenly Father, who sent His Son to bear your sin and loves you infinitely more than anyone else ever could, treat you worse than a selfish human being?

If the Lord hasn't already supplied your need by grace, your faith can't make Him do it. Contrary to popular belief, faith does not move God. He's not the one who's stuck! Neither does He need to "move." God has already done everything! The Lord is never taken by surprise because He established the supply long before you ever had the need. It's not like He has to go out and do something to provide your answer. Since He's already done His part, you don't have to beg and plead.

Chapter 4

The Model for Prayer

After this manner therefore pray ye: Our Father which art in heaven, Hallowed be thy name.

Matthew 6:9

The Lord was giving us a model for prayer, not something to repeat! If you are reciting the words of the "The Lord's Prayer," you're just soothing your conscience. Your feeling of *Man, I'm really observing my religious duty!* is all you're getting out of it because merely speaking these words doesn't earn you anything from God. This is nothing more than the vain repetition Jesus taught against in Matthew 6:7.

Jesus was communicating scriptural principles through this model prayer. You're supposed to begin by entering into His presence thanking, praising, and blessing Him (Ps. 100:4).

Every one of us has been guilty of entering into our Father's presence with a sense of unworthiness, saying, "God, I know I haven't prayed. I'm not loving the way I should. I didn't do this or that." We come in concerned, dominated, and focused on our failures instead of His goodness. The Father doesn't like His children approaching Him that way.

God's not mad at you! He took all of His anger out on His own Son two thousand years ago at the cross. Now you can approach Him without fear, based on what Christ has done. God's just glad to hear from you. He's not going to upbraid you. He isn't like that! There's simply no need to be afraid of your loving heavenly Father! If you feel like you're so sorry, then praise Him for the fact that He loves such a sorry person as you! Instead of focusing on your unworthiness, thank God for His goodness!

> **Instead of focusing on your unworthiness, thank God for His goodness!**

Death and life are in the power of the tongue....

Proverbs 18:21

Many Christians who think they're praying are really just griping, murmuring, and complaining. They don't realize that even in prayer, their words produce either death or life. Instead of getting the answers to their problems, they're actually energizing and strengthening their problems to continue dominating their lives! God's not pleased with that. You can't spend five seconds in faith and forty-five minutes in unbelief and negativity and then they ask, "Why am I not encouraged?" That's not an encouraging prayer! When you pray, it's important to have an attitude of gratitude. Start with praise, and you'll be releasing life!

Manifesting Heaven on Earth

Thy kingdom come. Thy will be done in earth, as it is in heaven.

Matthew 6:10

Jesus continued to praise God, declaring, "Father, I know that it's Your will for things to be done on earth the way they are in heaven." In heaven, there's no sickness. Therefore, it's not God's will for you to be sick. There's no poverty in heaven. So, it's not God's will for you to be poor here on earth. In the presence of the Lord, there is abundant joy, shouting, singing, praising, and worshiping. That's what heaven is like, and it's how He expects us to be here on earth! We should pray that what's already waiting for us in heaven would begin to manifest here in our lives on earth.

Take It!

Give us this day our daily bread.

Matthew 6:11

Notice that verse 11 isn't a question, because there's no question mark at the end. It's not saying, "O God, I know I don't deserve it, but would You please give me a crumb so I won't starve and perish today?" No! Providing meals is just part of the family relationship. Children expect their moms and dads to meet their needs. It's familiarity with their parents' love that makes them bold in their approach.

God wants us to be this way with Him! He desires all believers to be so familiar with His love that their approach toward Him is bold (Heb. 4:16). He yearns for His children to believe that all the provision they need has already been made.

Not many Christians approach God this way. We need to just take advantage of what He's already done and appropriate it!

Forgiven & Delivered

And forgive us our debts, as we forgive our debtors. And lead us not into temptation....

Matthew 6:12–13

I've hinted at this earlier in the booklet, but you need to understand that once you've believed and received the Lord, your sins are forgiven—past, present, and future. And, of course, He won't lead us into temptation! What loving Father would? Jesus spoke these things in Matthew 6 *before* the cross and resurrection. He was led into temptation on our behalf and overcame the devil (Matt. 4:1–11). If you are being led into temptation, you can be sure that it isn't God (James 1:13–14). In light of this truth, you can pray, "Father, I know it's not Your will for me to be tempted." That's fine.

> *But deliver us from evil: For thine is the kingdom, and the power, and the glory, for ever. Amen.*
>
> Matthew 6:13

Through faith in Christ, we transferred kingdoms. Jesus has already delivered us out of the kingdom of darkness and set us in the kingdom of light (Col. 1:13). The evil one lost his legal hold on us completely, and we now belong to our loving heavenly Father. For this, we praise Him. Hallelujah!

Christ's model prayer started with praise, *"Our Father which art in heaven, Hallowed be thy name,"* and ended with praise, *"For thine is the kingdom, and the power, and the glory, for ever. Amen"* (Matt. 6:9, 13). This is what I like to call the

> **Jesus has already delivered us out of the kingdom of darkness and set us in the kingdom of light.**

"Sandwich Technique." Start your prayer thanking Him, praising Him, and declaring how big He is. Then, slide in your petition, and end by praising Him some more. When you approach God with your request by slipping it in between two healthy slices of praise and thanksgiving, you'll find that you don't really have that much to ask Him for.

Chapter 5

Jesus—The Only Mediator

Most Christians believe that the only difference between the Old Testament and the New is one blank page in the Bible. They don't understand that the establishment of the New Covenant made a huge difference in the way everything works—including prayer!

> *I exhort therefore, that, first of all, supplications, prayers, intercessions, and giving of thanks, be made for all men; For kings, and for all that are in authority; that we may lead a quiet and peaceable life in all godliness and honesty. For this is good and acceptable in the sight of God our Saviour; Who will have all men to be saved, and to come unto the knowledge of the truth. **For there is one God, and one mediator between God and men, the man Christ Jesus.***"

1 Timothy 2:1–5

In the New Covenant, Jesus is the only mediator that stands between God the Father and mankind.

If you pray, "O God, please have mercy. Don't pour out your wrath!" you have just pushed Jesus aside and declared, "Lord, I know You atoned for us and that You dealt with sin. The Word says that You are the only mediator, but I think I can help. It's also going to take my pleading and interceding to make things right." You're trying to add to what Jesus has already done! Jesus + anything = nothing. Jesus + nothing = everything.

Ask, Seek, Knock

Jesus paid for our sins <u>and</u> satisfied God's wrath, but the church as a whole doesn't understand this yet. We still perceive God like He was in the Old Testament—angry. We think we must intercede to stop Him from doing what He really wants to do, which is to judge people for their sins. Many of us believe we still need to beg and plead with God for His mercy. That's absolutely wrong! God's Word in the New Testament reveals the depth of His love and forgiveness through Christ.

After giving the parable contrasting God with the friend (Luke 11:5–8), Jesus immediately pressed His point:

And I say unto you, Ask, and it shall be given you; seek, and ye shall find; knock, and it shall be opened unto you. For every one that asketh receiveth; and he that seeketh findeth; and to him that knocketh it shall be opened.

Luke 11:9–10

Then Jesus illustrated this truth even further by using the same logic with another human relationship.

If a son shall ask bread of any of you that is a father, will he give him a stone? or if he ask a fish, will he for a fish give him a serpent? Or if he shall ask an egg, will he offer him a scorpion? If ye then, being evil, know how to give good gifts unto your children: how much more shall your heavenly Father give the Holy Spirit to them that ask him?

Luke 11:11–13

If you wouldn't even consider treating your children so cruelly, why do you think God would refuse or even hesitate to meet your need? On the contrary, *"if you then, being evil, know how to give good gifts to your children,* **how much more** *will your heavenly Father give the Holy Spirit to those who ask Him?" (NKJV).*

Chapter 6

A Ploy of the Devil

D uring an all-night prayer meeting one time, when we bombarded the gates of heaven, I remember beating the wall and screaming, "God, if You loved the people in Arlington, Texas, half as much as I do, we'd have revival!" Immediately, my "lightning-fast" mind realized that there was something seriously wrong with my theology. I stopped dead in my tracks and said, "That's not right!" But this is where most "intercessors" are today.

Intercessors plead with the Lord, praying, "O God, please love these people as much as I do." You wouldn't use those exact words, but it's what you're doing. You believe God is angry, and He'd just let people die and go to hell if it weren't for your great prayers. Apart from you, God wouldn't heal anybody. You think your begging is making Him turn and extend mercy. Nothing could be farther from the truth!

God loves people infinitely more than you do! If you want to see your country turned around or someone saved, healed, and delivered, it's because God Himself has already touched your heart that you even have that desire. It's definitely not human nature! Man's nature is to be selfish and not care for anyone but himself. If you have compassion to see others touched, it's because God is already working on you. He's the one who gave you that compassion. He stirred you up, not so you could plead with Him to become as merciful as you are, but that motivated by love, you would start releasing the power of God by going out and doing something about it.

Claiming Others for Salvation

The Holy Spirit doesn't move independent of people. God has told believers to go out and heal the sick, cleanse the lepers, raise the dead, and cast out demons. Instead of doing what He's commanded us to do, we're asking God to do what He told us to do. It's not time for Him to pour out His Spirit—He already has. He's dwelling in every born-again believer. We just need to start speaking the truth and releasing the power of the Spirit to others!

> **The Holy Spirit doesn't move independent of people.**

Literally thousands of people have come up to me and asked, "How come so-and-so isn't saved? I've been claiming them in prayer for over twenty years now, and God hasn't answered my prayer!" What a sorry attitude!

And they said, Believe on the Lord Jesus Christ, and thou shalt be saved, and thy house.

Acts 16:31

This scripture from the Philippian jailer passage is commonly taught, "Claim your relatives—your whole house—for salvation." You can't "claim" someone else's salvation. This verse doesn't mean that. It's saying, "Believe on the Lord Jesus Christ and you'll be saved—your house will too, if they believe. It'll work for anyone!"

If "claiming" another's salvation really worked, then we should quit teaching anything else and focus on this one thing. Organize the churches to "claim" all of their relatives. Then, once they're saved, immediately lead them in "claiming" all of theirs too. If this were true, we could "claim" and win the whole world in no time flat! This simply cannot be done, because each individual must personally believe in Christ for themselves.

Consider the Fruit

Satan is behind much of the teaching on "prayer" floating around in the body of Christ today. Consider the fruit. Christians are being driven into their prayer closets, not valuing what the Lord has done, trying to take His position as mediator, begging Him not to pour out wrath He no longer has, crying out for the Holy Spirit who's already been poured out, and pleading with Him to become as merciful as they are. Meanwhile, their family, co-workers, and neighbors are going to hell.

You ought to be out there speaking God's Word and demonstrating the power of God:

And [Jesus] said unto [His disciples], Go ye into all the world, and preach the gospel to every creature. He that believeth and is baptized shall be saved; but he that believeth not shall be damned. And these signs shall follow them that believe; In my name shall they cast out devils; they shall speak with new tongues; They shall take up serpents; and if they drink any deadly thing, it shall not hurt them; they shall lay hands on the sick, and they shall recover.

Mark 16:15–18

What a ploy of the devil to get Christians to sidestep this Great Commission and distract them with "interceding" in their prayer closets!

Chapter 7

No New Testament Model

Jesus never organized "prayer warriors" and "intercessors" the way it's modeled today. He never sent His disciples out to pray over a city in order to "prepare the ground." He did send them forth in advance to publicize His coming, because they didn't have radio, television, newspapers, internet, social media, billboards, and so on back then. These disciples spread the word of His miracles, but Jesus never ordained any "prayer warriors" or "intercessors." There's simply no scriptural New Testament model for such things.

The logic behind all of this today states that there are demonic powers holding certain areas captive. Before going in and preaching the Gospel, the "strongman" must be bound and his power broken. Although that sounds "spiritual," Jesus didn't do it this way and neither did Paul. Am I disputing the fact that there are demonic powers at work in the world today? No. I've seen demons come out of people. I'm also fully aware that there are demonic powers over cities.

Demons are present even in church services! Some may say, "Well, they shouldn't be. Plead the blood and keep them out!" You can't do that! Satan attended the Last Supper with Jesus (John 13:27). If Christ couldn't keep Satan away from His communion table, what makes you think you can?

What about Spiritual Warfare?

In Acts 19, when Paul dealt with Diana of the Ephesians, a false god, multitudes of people regularly came to worship her image (which was reputed to have fallen down from Jupiter) in the temple at Ephesus. Paul never told the disciples to pray against her, never led a praise service to bind her, and never did what modern-day Christians call "spiritual warfare" or "spiritual mapping." They didn't go back into the history of Ephesus to repent and apologize for all the different sins so that God could finally move.

What did Paul and his co-laborers do? They preached the truth that there's no other God but God the Father and His Son—the Lord Jesus Christ! In a relatively short period of time, the entire worship of Diana of the Ephesians was on the verge of being completely abandoned, because someone dared to tell the people the truth. The subsequent religious, political, and primarily economic aftershocks caused Paul to be nearly stoned to death (Acts 19:23–41). Am I arguing that there wasn't a demonic power operating through this worship of Diana of the Ephesians? No, I believe there was. However, Paul and his companions didn't deal with it in prayer. They boldly spoke the truth of God's Word with Holy Spirit power demonstrated to the people.

Chapter 8

Speak to Your Mountain

Mark 11 contains some tremendous lessons about how to receive from God in prayer:

> *And on the morrow, when they were come from Bethany, he was hungry: And seeing a fig tree afar off having leaves, he came, if haply he might find any thing thereon: and when he came to it, he found nothing but leaves; for the time of figs was not yet. And Jesus answered and said unto it, No man eat fruit of thee hereafter for ever. And his disciples heard it.*
>
> Mark 11:12–14

Although Jesus spoke to this fig tree and instantly it was done, the results weren't visible until twelve hours later. Sometimes it takes time for what God has already accomplished to manifest itself in the physical realm.

And Peter calling to remembrance saith unto him, Master, behold, the fig tree which thou cursedst is withered away.

Mark 11:21

Peter was shocked the next morning when he saw that fig tree! In reading the Scriptures, we often have a tendency to overlook how it must have felt for those living it. You'd be pretty impressed if, as we were walking along, I commanded a tree "Die, in the name of Jesus!" and the next day you found it shriveled up dead. You'd say something, wouldn't you? Peter didn't just mention this—he was overwhelmed: "Jesus, look at this fig tree!"

The Lord used this teachable moment to illustrate how prayer works:

And Jesus answering saith unto them, Have faith in God.

Mark 11:22

This happened through faith in God. Faith is a powerful force, but you must believe in order to reap its benefits.

For verily I say unto you, That whosoever shall say unto this mountain, Be thou removed, and be thou cast into the sea; and shall not doubt in his heart, but shall believe that those things which he saith shall come to pass; he shall have whatsoever he saith.

Mark 11:23

The Lord commands us to speak to our mountain. The "mountain" represents whatever our problem is. This is a truth about prayer that most people have missed. They speak to God about their mountain instead of speaking to their mountain about God! We've got to declare, "Sickness, disease, poverty, death—be gone in the name of Jesus!" not "God, I have this mountain. Would You please move it for me?" The Lord told *you* to talk to *it*, not to Him. Whatever *it* is, have faith in God and *speak* to it!

> *Therefore I say unto you, What things soever ye desire, when ye pray, believe that ye receive them, and ye shall have them.*
>
> Mark 11:24

I want you to notice what Jesus was saying here as He explained what He did to the fig tree. He took His authority and called it believing, and He called speaking to the problem "prayer." This is another radical truth that most people miss about prayer. Jesus said to believe that you have received God's answer the instant you pray (speak to the mountain), and you shall (future tense) see the visible manifestation of it.

As you speak to your mountain, you are cooperating with an important spiritual law and expediting the manifestation of your answer!

How the Kingdom Works

Many people struggle with what I'm teaching, wondering, *How can I believe? I have pain in my body right now, but you're telling me to believe that I'm healed without any physical evidence of it.* Others respond, "Oh, I understand! You're saying to act like it's so, when it really isn't so, and then it'll become so!" No, that's not what I'm teaching. I'm not encouraging you into some "mind game" of trying to believe something is real when it isn't so that it'll become real. I'm challenging you to look beyond just the natural realm.

God is a Spirit (John 4:24). When He moves, He does so in the spirit realm. The very moment you were born again, you received everything you need in spiritual form inside your spirit. You have the same virtue, anointing, and power that raised Jesus Christ from the dead (Eph. 1:19–20; Rom. 8:1). Therefore, it's not a question of whether God has given it. He's done everything He's going to do about your miracle. He gave the command, released His power, and it's a done deal!

"But I need it out here in my body," someone might say. Faith is the bridge from the spiritual realm into the physical realm. It's how what has already happened in the spirit transfers over into the natural. Faith gives substance to things hoped for

Faith is the bridge from the spiritual realm into the physical realm.

and evidence—tangibility, physical proof—to something unseen (Heb. 11:1).

This is how the kingdom works. We've made it too hard, praying, "O God, here's my need. If You love me, do something!" When nothing happens, we become bitter at God and wonder, *Why haven't You done anything?* We don't always see it manifest because we haven't learned how to receive. It's not because God didn't answer! He has given us the power, but so many of us are ignorant of how it works.

"Are you saying it's my fault?" Yes, I am. Some people become very upset when they hear this and think, *You're condemning me!* No, I'm not. I'm just letting you know that if somebody missed it, it wasn't God!

Knowing that God is always faithful blesses me! He's not choosing to heal this one and leave another sick, prosper that one and ignore someone else, or give joy to that one and not another. This concept that "God just wanted to bless that person and make this other one miserable" isn't true. He's not like that! He wants every one of us to have health, prosperity, joy, blessing, peace, and happiness. It's just that not everybody receives it. This isn't because God is not faithful to give, but rather, not everyone knows how to go from "amen" to "there it is." It's really that simple.

You've got the anointing of God to heal the sick, cleanse the lepers, and raise the dead. If you aren't seeing it manifest, it's not God's giver that is broken but your receiver that needs to be turned on and tuned in. Get into the Word, and then use it to speak to your mountain!

Your Results Will Improve

God is using imperfect people. We'd all see greater and quicker manifestations if we weren't so full of unbelief! It's a miracle we see anything happen while bathing our minds in murder, adultery, and sexual immorality for "entertainment" and listening to the (bad) "news" each day. We're baptized in unbelief!

Since Jesus has to use imperfect vessels like you and me, sometimes His power doesn't come into manifestation as quickly. Each of us has some unbelief and other junk that hasn't been worked out yet—but don't let that stop you from doing it! Your conductivity for God's power often increases through use. Don't just give up if you try a few times and don't yet see the results you desire. Even Jesus was limited in what He could do in His own hometown because of their unbelief (Matt. 13:58). Keep at it!

Your conductivity for God's power often increases through use.

As you begin to understand, believe, and practice some of these things, your results will greatly improve!

Chapter 9

The Variable

D aniel's example clearly illustrates God's faithfulness to always answer prayer. He prayed two different times, in Daniel 9 and 10, and received two different results. God answered both prayers instantly, but the first took approximately three minutes before he received an answer, and the other took three weeks. Let's read in Daniel 10 to find out why:

> *But the prince of the kingdom of Persia withstood me [the angelic messenger] one and twenty days: but, lo, Michael, one of the chief princes, came to help me; and I remained there with the kings of Persia.*

Daniel 10:13

The angelic messenger told Daniel what the holdup had been—demonic opposition. Jude 9 and Revelation 12:7 reveal Michael to be an archangel. Notice how the messenger had been withstood since the first day Daniel prayed. God had instantly responded, but the messenger needed Michael's help to break through the demonic opposition with Daniel's answer.

Many people don't understand that we're living in a world that has demonic opposition. They think that if God sends an answer, there can be no hindrances. Of course, God is greater than the devil, but Satan can hinder Him if a physical person cooperates and gives him authority to do so. Things don't work instantly and automatically just because they're God's will and you prayed for it.

However, that is not an indictment on God. He is always constant! According to His Word—which is all we can base our lives on—we declare, "By His stripes, we were healed" (1 Pet. 2:24). He would have all to be healed of their sickness and disease. That's what the Bible teaches. Therefore, the variable isn't the Lord—it's the devil! God answered both of Daniel's prayers the moment he prayed, but Satan opposed and delayed the answer from the second prayer.

Now, many people erroneously believe that the devil is infallible and faithful all the time. They think he never misses a beat! Although they might not admit it, that's truly what they believe! People have often told me how they've done everything they know to do but still aren't sure if God will come through for them. However, if they do the slightest thing wrong, they have no doubt whatsoever that Satan will get them every time. These Christians have more faith in the devil than they do in God!

You need to know that Satan blows it lots of times. Why didn't he fight the prayer in Daniel 9? He was probably preoccupied elsewhere when Daniel prayed the first time. However, after Daniel received a tremendous answer and revelation, Satan assigned a major demonic power to make sure Daniel didn't get any other prayers through.

Take Authority and Shorten the Time

As an Old Testament saint, Daniel didn't have any authority over the devil. Therefore, he couldn't rebuke the demonic entity called *"the prince of the kingdom of Persia"* (Dan. 10:13). Even if Daniel had known that the problem between chapters 9 and 10 was demonic, he wouldn't have been able to do anything about it. However, as New Covenant believers, we do have authority over the devil (Luke 9:1).

When you know in your heart that God has already given the answer to you in the spirit realm, you don't have to hold on three weeks—or any length of time—for it to manifest in the physical realm. As a believer in Jesus Christ, take your authority, and command the devil to leave. Instead of telling God about it, speak directly to the problem. Then act on God's Word. Don't just sit idly by, waiting—do something!

It's Up to You!

If you're praying according to God's will, He always answers your prayers instantly (1 John 5:14–15), but you don't always immediately know what the hindrance might be. Use wisdom and pray in the Spirit until God leads you in a certain direction.

Sometimes it takes a period of time for you to discover what the problem is. Once you find out, take your authority over it. This will shorten the amount of time it takes to see it manifest. It's basically up to you how quickly you see your answers to prayer!

> **If you're praying according to God's will, He always answers your prayers instantly.**

Jesus used this same strategy while praying for a blind man (Mark 8:22–26). He took the man out of town, prayed for him, and then asked what he saw. Some would say, "Well, that's unbelief!" No, Jesus wasn't asking, "Did it work?" He knew God had given. The reason He took the man out of town in the first place was because Bethsaida was so full of unbelief.

Jesus said, "Woe unto thee, Bethsaida! for if the mighty works had been done in Tyre and Sidon, which have been done in you, they had a great while ago repented…" (Luke 10:13).

Bethsaida was one of the most unbelieving cities Jesus ever visited. He had to take this man by the hand and lead him away from the unbelief of the people in town.

Even though Jesus had the man out of the town, He knew He hadn't gotten all of the town out of the man! The Lord perceived that there were still some hindrances of unbelief in him. Jesus prayed, knowing His Father had released the power. Therefore, He wasn't asking "Did it work?" but rather "Have you received? Are you still having problems?" The Lord confronted the physical problem head on and looked squarely at it.

When the man only manifested a partial healing, Jesus prayed for him again. That would get Him kicked out of most Bible colleges today, because "it's not faith to ask for something twice!" The Lord didn't ask for anything twice. He believed and received it the first time. The second time, He took His spiritual power and authority and used it, and the man saw clearly. This is how we ought to do it.

Conclusion

As I said at the beginning of this book, this is neither *The Only Way to Pray* nor *You're All Wrong If You Don't Pray This Way.* This book has been about *A Better Way to Pray.* I've done all the things that I said were wrong, and yet I still loved God and He loved me. But since I've been praying the way I've taught in this book, I've seen great improvement in the results I get.

My prayer for you is that the Lord will take these things I've shared and bring you into a new understanding of what prayer is and how your prayers can be more effective. I believe the Lord will use these truths to bring you out of any "religious" traditions that make the Word of God of no effect in your life. You'll experience the freedom and joy that knowing God in spirit and truth brings.

And as you receive and these truths set you free, I pray that the Lord will grant you opportunities to share these things with others so they too can begin experiencing *A Better Way to Pray*!

Receive Jesus as Your Savior

C hoosing to receive Jesus Christ as your Lord and Savior is the most important decision you'll ever make!

God's Word promises, *"That if thou shalt confess with thy mouth the Lord Jesus, and shalt believe in thine heart that God hath raised him from the dead, thou shalt be saved. For with the heart man believeth unto righteousness; and with the mouth confession is made unto salvation"* (Rom. 10:9–10). *"For whosoever shall call upon the name of the Lord shall be saved"* (Rom. 10:13). By His grace, God has already done everything to provide salvation. Your part is simply to believe and receive.

Pray out loud: "Jesus, I confess that You are my Lord and Savior. I believe in my heart that God raised You from the dead. By faith in Your Word, I receive salvation now. Thank You for saving me."

The very moment you commit your life to Jesus Christ, the truth of His Word instantly comes to pass in your spirit. Now that you're born again, there's a brand-new you!

Please contact us and let us know that you've prayed to receive Jesus as your Savior. We'd like to send you some free materials to help you on your new journey. Call our Helpline: **719-635-1111** (available 24 hours a day, seven days a week) to speak to a staff member who is here to help you understand and grow in your new relationship with the Lord.

Welcome to your new life!

Receive the Holy Spirit

As His child, your loving heavenly Father wants to give you the supernatural power you need to live a new life. *"For every one that asketh receiveth; and he that seeketh findeth; and to him that knocketh it shall be opened...how much more shall your heavenly Father give the Holy Spirit to them that ask him?"* (Luke 11:10–13).

All you have to do is ask, believe, and receive!

Pray this: "Father, I recognize my need for Your power to live a new life. Please fill me with Your Holy Spirit. By faith, I receive it right now. Thank You for baptizing me. Holy Spirit, You are welcome in my life."

Congratulations! Now you're filled with God's supernatural power.

Some syllables from a language you don't recognize will rise up from your heart to your mouth (1 Cor. 14:14). As you speak them out loud by faith, you're releasing God's power from within and building yourself up in the spirit (1 Cor. 14:4). You can do this whenever and wherever you like.

It doesn't really matter whether you felt anything or not when you prayed to receive the Lord and His Spirit. If you believed in your heart that you received, then God's Word promises you did. *"Therefore I say unto you, What things soever ye desire, when ye pray, believe that ye receive them, and ye shall have them"* (Mark 11:24). God always honors His Word—believe it!

We would like to rejoice with you and help you understand more fully what has taken place in your life! Please contact us to let us know that you've prayed to be filled with the Holy Spirit and to receive some free materials we have for you. Call our Helpline: **719-635-1111** (available 24 hours a day, seven days a week).

Call for Prayer

If you need prayer for any reason, you can call our Helpline, 24 hours a day, seven days a week at **719-635-1111**. A trained prayer minister will answer your call and pray with you.

Every day, we receive testimonies of healings and other miracles from our Helpline, and we are ministering God's nearly-too-good-to-be-true message of the Gospel to more people than ever. So, I encourage you to call today!

About the Author

Andrew Wommack's life was forever changed the moment he encountered the supernatural love of God on March 23, 1968. As a renowned Bible teacher and author, Andrew has made it his mission to change the way the world sees God.

Andrew's vision is to go as far and deep with the Gospel as possible. His message goes far through the *Gospel Truth* television program, which is available to nearly half the world's population. The message goes deep through discipleship at Charis Bible College, headquartered in Woodland Park, Colorado. Founded in 1994, Charis has campuses across the United States and around the globe.

Andrew also has an extensive library of teaching materials in print, audio, and video—most of which can be accessed for free from his website: awmi.net.

Contact Information

Andrew Wommack Ministries, Inc.

PO Box 3333
Colorado Springs, CO 80934-3333
info@awmi.net
awmi.net

Helpline: 719-635-1111 (available 24/7)

Charis Bible College

info@charisbiblecollege.org
844-360-9577
CharisBibleCollege.org

For a complete list of all of our offices,
visit **awmi.net/contact-us**.

Connect with us on social media.

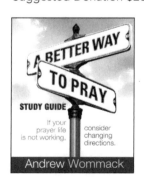